SIREN

SIREN

Kateri Lanthier

THE POETRY IMPRINT AT VÉHICULE PRESS

Published with the generous assistance of The Canada Council for the
Arts and the Canada Book Fund of the Department of Canadian Heritage.

Funded by the Government of Canada
Financé par le gouvernement du Canada | Canadä

SIGNAL EDITIONS EDITOR: CARMINE STARNINO

Cover design: David Drummond
Photo of the author by Gregory Sinclair
Set in Filosofia and Minion by Simon Garamond
Printed by Marquis Book Printing Inc.

Dépôt légal, Library and Archives Canada and the
Bibliothèque national du Québec, second trimester 2017.

LIBRARY AND ARCHIVES CANADA CATALOGUING IN PUBLICATION

Lanthier, Kateri, author
Siren / Kateri Lanthier.

Poems.
Issued in print and electronic formats.
ISBN 978-1-55065-466-0 (softcover). – ISBN 978-1-55065-473-8 (EPUB)

I. Title.

PS8623.A69878S57 2017   C811'.6   C2016-907356-4
C2016-907357-2

Published by Véhicule Press, Montréal, Québec, Canada
www.vehiculepress.com

Distribution in Canada by LitDistCo
www.litdistco.ca

Distributed in the U.S. by Independent Publishers Group
www.ipgbook.com

Printed in Canada on FSC certified paper.

For the Lanthier line:
Edwin (Ned), Philip, Jim

CONTENTS

One

Two

Three

*I'm neither the loosening of song nor the close-drawn
tent of music;
I'm the sound, simply, of my own breaking.*

– GHALIB,
translated by Aijaz Ahmad and Adrienne Rich

*First things: lost. The milky saucer,
of last things a siren.*

JOHN THOMPSON, Ghazal XXVIII, *Stilt Jack*

One

Siren

I was the waif in the snowbank of the banquet hall parking lot.
A voluptuous stray. A bravura drunk. My thoughts encrypted in sugar.

Chiming through my rain-streaked gaze, the hues of this week's cocktail:
Curaçao blues, maraschino rage, olive, lime cordial, *not bitter*.

Unplugged from the folk circuit, unhinged by your grin.
When the heat deigns to return, the extremities sing pain.

The perimeter keeps expanding. Shots ricochet round the arch.
Catch me, catch me, if you must! Bake me into the Earth's crust.

I clawed you from the rock and now you glisten on my finger.
In the marble at your temples, I can trace the throb of doubt.

All night the blind truck-river-road courses past my house.
Sirens swim the butterfly to comfort each shipwreck.

Merrily, Merrily, Merrily, Merrily ✓

I'm stamen-stained and pistil-whipped, forced to bloom by heart.
Let's sew your shadow back on in the situation room.

I magicked you out of the morning roar. I sang you out of my hair.
All this time I've only known you by your *nom de guerre*.

Your story has gone viral. An epic lie, pandemic.
We had to go extra innings in an overlit diamond ring.

A babyless bathwater moon over The Silver (*burnt-out*) Dollar Room.
How that a life was but a flower. You knew me by my petals.

Give me your educated guess. I feel embedded in ice.
All thoughts, all pleasures, all delights must end in freezing rain.

Not for all the tea in teacher, all the harm in charm.
I can't get warm this year, so I must wear the living room.

Last laugh to the laugh track that will outlast us all.
My red lipstick: safety feature, sign of poison, bull's-eye?

Junk Science

I plan to leave this party soon unless they lower the tone.
Each word of yours is an empty calorie sprinkled with pink sea salt.

Enough of your sympathetic magic, junk science and false gods!
Poor bees. They tried and tried but failed to keep their deaths from us.

Oh, every snowflake's a unique star, a fallen fingerprint.
And what do we do with these babies? We plow 'em like dirt and plant cars.

Your protests are as wind chimes when the hurricane blows in.
While we plié or chest-pump, the ice storm antlers each branch.

Denim sings the workers' blues, a French folk song *de Nîmes*.
In case of emergency, tap the glass and your promises will shatter.

You can get all the news that stays news from a fashion magazine.
Denim goes with everything: diamonds, bent rebar, blood lust.

Baby Grand ✓

But I followed instructions! *Wring blood from a stone and use the drops as lip gloss.*
My new job is branding mascara. This one's called "The Tracks of My Tears."

At the baby grand, my pearly whites dissolved to box-office poison.
Sawzall, Adderall, bias-cut satin: recipe for trouble.

You can let yourself down from the ceiling. My name is no longer Miss Muffet.
Now I'm known as Queen Charlotte the Second. In my memoirs, your chapter is "Some Pig."

A thousand years after disco died, we gaze at the glittering sphere.
Every ceiling fixture we own is a *folie de grandeur*.

I might have known we'd come unglued in the Palace of Particleboard.
The baptismal river of tears flows to an azure ocean playground.

From Formula One to formulaic before the engine cooled.
Headless torso, knees and toes in the bullet-ridden sky.

Round three and the love is off. My fingertips are numbskulls.
A right-handed woman is always in search of a missing right-hand glove.

There Was Something in My Dream About a Cat

I'm a nymph in the cumulonimbus, a mortar shell in the café.
You gave me a quivery unfocussed kiss. The dream-cat leapt from
   your head.

Our every kiss a power surge that sparked a rolling blackout.
Where the bee sucks, there suck I. Swooning astride the no-fault line.

How *was* it? Like trying to speak with dignity into a megaphone.
Like trying to hide your tears while strapped into the driver's seat.

Audition here, coquettes and wags with the infernal cast of mind.
Meet me on the mondegreen, meet me in the jet stream.

The coral has osteoporosis. Don't wake the infant snow squall.
You think cats don't have shoulders? Just watch one muscle the door.

You can tug my forelock and lead me to slaughter but you can't
   make me drink.
March rolls out the beige carpet. Roll the barrel over the falls.

Uncontrolled Burn ✓

If you drop your weapons'-grade handshake, I'll carry your kiss to
    the car.
Court controversy, skip the altar. What will survive of us is Spring.

Charged particles sparkle in your glass and lengthen your eyelashes.
Despite your reassurances, I wouldn't call us a controlled burn.

Wind rose while we circumnavigated. Night slammed us against the
    sea wall.
I wear this mourning jewellery: your book splayed over my breasts.

The sky fell and chilled in a sweet-freeze bitter on the tongue.
The trees were empty-nesters. Cradles landed on the lawn.

The birds of Deutsche Grammophon pine for the birds of field
    recordings.
Ask the cat that climbs the tree to speak about roots and wings.

It's cops on testosterone at the school. It's your five-year-old spelling
    "F-O-R-E-N-S-I-C-S."
One week later, the party balloons are guests still riding their high.

Easy Street

You won't end up on Easy Street if you wear that hair-of-the-dog
   shirt.
No amount of rehearsed apology will get you to Carnegie Hall.

We're bittersweet? Then let me count the ways, I mean, the petals.
O let me plant my kisses all along your neck of the woods.

You say you'll be my mirror. You're more like my indoor plunge pool.
When I finally looked you in the eye, sorrow skipped a beat.

7 a.m., looking eastward: Socked in the eye by a rose bouquet.
7 p.m.: My heart's on ice. I'm buying that sunset a drink.

The furthest thing from your mind is closer than it appears.
The many-navelled mattress doesn't care which side is up.

And every dinosaur was just a lizard who spoke Latin.
Curiosity killed the Cheshire-Cat. Now I wear his grin.

Asleep, fat cat's a half moon; skinny one, a new.
Keep me as an illegal pet. My thoughts are actionable.

No accounting for taste? Actually, it's all too easy.
It's all too easy to follow your cyber-trail through the bushes.

Ah, teeny birds *that slepen al the nyght with open ye…*
What are their screen names? Jessica, Jennifer and Ingenuous.

Splendor, Good Cheer and Mirth—two-thirds of the Graces are
   pleasant?
Give me compelling melancholy. Not butterfly-rose tattoos.

Maple schemes to be a redhead; birch and aspen, to be blonde.
Playing all week in the Pine Gloom Room: Your Melancholy Baby.

Period Drama ✓

Gravity's centred ache, tears, then blasé with blood.
Maps left on mattresses: clues to my blood.

Tender nipples, hot buttons, the temper, the flood.
Late start at 13, then four decades of blood.

3 x nine-months' break. Babies slipped out in blood.
The womb contracts at breastfeeding, contract of blood.

Enormous tiny children, huge privacy loss.
A surge! White knit blankets. The running to blood.

Red weather. Mothership of pad, clips, garter belt.
The arcane how-they-coped, metal sharks' teeth with blood.

Once-a-month Celtic witch, I must sing of my blood.
Pass the tampon baton. Raise a cup to this blood.

Florillegal

Peonies. Their blowsiness defines "unfairly beautiful."
What frightens me is baby's breath in hospital gift shops.

Saplings shocked pink by a cold snap are pleased and scared
    pubescents.
My friends are walking backlit past a burn-victim birch.

Cold and wet, March lion mewls all night under the front porch.
Cradling newborn leaves, every maple's a weeping willow.

Costly scent, cheap sentiment. You'll pay and pay and pay.
Better to wear the ambiance of woodsmoke, snow and oak.

I've a bird's eye view of the squirrel's eye view of the tulip's
    periscope.
This four-alarm forsythia shocks the city without fail.

Needle lace, bonsai, rondels, haiku, knot gardens.
Admire, fear and covet every sign of bottled desire.

"*Ne m'oubliez pas*, calqued from the French, first used in English
    c. 1532."
Sweet Wiki-wildflowers. Blue-eyed forgive-and-forget-me-nots.

My Red Hair √

Was it '70s film stock that first lit the flare?
Blonde-haired babe, auburn kid. Now I choose my red hair.

Small-screen siren comedienne, curled-lip long-stemmed rose.
Unbeliever! Fingers fire-walk through my red hair.

Spray-painted for raves: silver nitrate, cyan, lime,
washed next day to ruby embers. Trash is treasure, my red hair.

Bookish kid, owlish adult. Did Lucy Maud miss *her* "e"?
Anne could burn down Green Gables with my red hair.

Postpartum red-handed, bleeding for what's gone and here.
Pale blue newborn eyes focus on my red hair.

Pin-ups: Garnet, Ruby, Beryl. Sardonic wise-crack Sardonyx.
Lust's objective correlative: my red hair.

Phoenix. Firebird. Plath. I will eat them like air.
Set your mouth near my temple. Fire-breathe my red hair.

Red Kat, October poet, you're not immortal Red Tārā.
The fire in snow, the flash in opal: my red hair.

Too Soon

Spring petal skirt-chasers caught the magnolia blushing.
Who'll bite? Your studded muscle-car tongue baits the gated
   community.

Baby acorn, what's this? You threw your hat in the ring too soon.
Every rubber duck's a miniature yellow submarine.

A cat's ears are its eyebrows. Our Lady of Perpetual Astonishment.
The road wears a long, unwinding ruff of Queen Anne's Lace.

Strike that matchless beauty from your mind. *as if that's possible*
To you, I was merely a paring of the Empress's fingernails.

Necrophiliac ventriloquism! Your practitioners are legion.
And now my thoughts are trembling like a toddler's lower lip.

Boots on the ground, dog in the fight, skin in the game.
To you, it's a bed of roses. To me, a crown of thorns.

The stars blaze on in re-run. We must stop clouding around.
I sing these songs all through the dark, after everyone's left.

When it comes to the heart, "benign neglect" can resemble criminal
   negligence.
You cannot throw yourself into the same lake twice.

Two

Fashion Advice For Eternity

Leave those Tiffany rings. They're a pile of cold cash.
Facile, faceted carbon copies.
Give us jewellery or give us death.
The Seven Cities of Cíbola, a Spanish fantasy,
led to ruined pueblos, disease, yes, death.
But here's what the A:shiwi do:
The Zuni jeweller takes a fingertip of shards
from a surgeon's tray of stars
and sets a miniature Thunderbird, Kachina dancer,
Knifewing, Roadrunner, face of the Sun
in spiny oyster, abalone, turquoise, onyx night
ringed by silver kicked from a horse's hoof
on your finger, by your breastbone, at your ear.

Heart Monitor

My blood is in a palace coup against my lungs,
Racing through the heart's hallways
The corridors of the powerless.

Oh, I contain multitudes, yes,
A throng of the mutinous. Ruby-throated
Clots in the bloodstream stole my breath.

Here I lie, untitled. *Unfinished work.*
Pale, bruise-eyed, nothing to see,
But an "art line" fireworks my veins

Blue, yellow, red! to the pretty screen.
That's my last duchess, over my shoulder,
Livestreaming spots of crimson joy.

It's cold in the gallery. Mint walls, peach "art"
(eternal still-life: the uprooted undead
drinking water through their veins)

That no one sees. All eyes on screen.
The resonance of emerald, the rush…
Remote heart monitor, cat on my lap,

Purrs to the nurse on another floor.
There, they never sleep, so I dream for them.
Their installation piece: The Scribbler.

Across the hall's The Scream. He has the view:
Ravine, icewater, the distaff drive
Where Trauma arrives.

Or perhaps I have the view: the lit-all-night
Stairwell, brick, snowflakes flying upwards.
Bent over my notes, what am I really?

The Lacemaker. My heart's apace.
I'll write to you until I lose
My sight, the thread and the current's flow.

A Colder Spring

Crocuses, you're down there somewhere,
but, sorry to say, I forgot you existed.
The New Ferocity gave me brain-freeze;
the continent a crystal skull of ice.
Across a gyre of debris-field waves,
your imperial purple has been dredged from floods.
Resolved into a dew, soaked earth overheats.

So it was with last spring with the cat. What cat?
I spent a week in and out of bed with death,
playing nurse or doctor in a backless gown,
hooked to a slow-drip icicle IV.
My sister brought crocuses to block the snow
of overbleached sheets, the view, my mirrored blank.
Name snipped off my wrist, I was free to walk.
At home, my kids swooped, captive songbirds.
Funeral or wedding march? I climbed stair-stop-stair.
And there on the bed was the cat. We have a *cat*?
I'd forgotten she existed. Only then could I melt.

Guanyin Lamp

A Guanyin lamp left burning in a closed storefront.
Light without mercy on your small right-hand finger,
On your head and broken finger.

Here's the boy, the girl, faces stroked by your robe.
You're a hollow never filled
And your face is serene.

The "Cries of the World" unheard behind plate glass.
Dust-streaked kitsch, you dream of sound.
I dream of our rescue.

All that's empty was once filled past the brim.
The fountains unstoppable—
Air, blood, song.

If I could rub your cheek, place a finger on your brow,
Find scrolled below the lotus the poems of—or—,
Not a worker's lament.

One of the numbered innumerable, faces lowered.
Compassion cast in clay.
The moon in tears.

Blanched pomegranate at your feet. Fish mid-leap.
Shipped by freighter, globe-poised Guanyin, unhearing…
Unbury me.

Walk me through the flames. We'll emerge soft and fearless
With a thousand arms each
And a mouth for every wound.

We'll perch on chemical clouds, rolling dragon dust.
Pain glazed from our lips.
The planet run to extremes.

An engine misfires. I rest my forehead on glass.
Moth-hearted, lost in adulthood,
Thirsty for light.

All the cries of the world! Something to sell, swallow, sorrow.
Your uncontrolled kindness
Rains on the void.

Emerald Table

Verum, sine mendacio, certum et verissimum

From gold chains of laburnum—sinuous, poisonous—
The God of Love leans out too far, drops every arrow in the waves
And ceases to exist.

Rings rollick on the surface in a diagram of hell.
A green-eyed map of pleasure-pain, iris-unique, torturous
Meditation circles.

My gaze drifts on the water as if on burning air.
Nessun maggior dolore che ricordarsi del tempo felice
ne la miseria…

You fanned my hair in red-gold rays. Bull's-eye. In one.
Your aim was true. You wrote the code, set flame and fired from the sun,
An elegant sharpshooter.

'Separate thou the earth from the fire, the subtile from the gross
  Sweetly with great indoustry.' In your liquid-bright glance
Lay a false economy,

My glistering, unlawful prize. Mad, you coaxed extravagance:
Dialogue by day and night, character and pixel, byte,
Fast-deleted scenes.

Independence declared, done. You closed my throat. The drug withdrawn.
Precious pet, gold-collared swan. Tricked-out diamonds in the blood.
Bubbles in a vein.

Eyebrow-arched, this Bridge of Sighs in Nowhere-by-the-Sea.
I lean over the emerald. Catch, cold waters. Kiss goodbye
Our disengagement ring.

Keeping Up

We are thrashing nerves with a fine façade.
Chocolate smudged everywhere. Foiled eggs
incubating below scatter rugs, magicians' cloths
snapped from beneath each meal.
Tumble-dried tears. Socks lying slain.

Our sugar-cookie house in crumbs,
gingerbread mattresses moldering.
The bubble reputation bursts in our South Sea tank
where iridescent fish goggle, glum
at their view of grey bark, grisaille sky.

Coffee on reheat in the unmade kitchen
where even the veins in lettuce reproach me.
I read the entrails of fingerpaint:
a gut-wrenching blue, that butchered sky.

Haiku

JUST SAYING (*FOR W.C.W.*)

Plums from the icebox?
Was he kidding? My teeth hurt.
Poets are liars.

FOR SAMUEL T.C.

This chilled patio
my Parnassus, this lime-juice
vodka my prison.

MARVELLOUS

Fog diffused the light.
We scattered night. Our sun stood
still. We'll make him run.

SEXT

What are you wearing?
Something that breathes: a dress
made of living doves.

ONE DAY I'LL WRITE AN ENGLYN

A red Welsh dragon
hunting red weather tigers:
this poem's sleeve tattoo.

IN GRATITUDE FOR *GARMENTS AGAINST WOMEN*

Anne Boyer, have you
sewn your French seam? Strawberries,
sugar. Silk. Sweat. Cream.

GATSBY

I long for a room.
You in a pink-cloud stanza
where we push and pull.

BOOK FORT

I hid in the bed
and read Anne Sexton.
#poetmotherconfessions

FORT BOOK (*FOR ROBARTS LIBRARY*)

Cherry blossoms blush
at stern library scholars.
Pink kisses concrete.

BYE, BYE, HAPPINESS

One cricket always
takes the lead, the mic, the love:
Sing, Buddy Holly.

LIMBIC

October borrows
September's leaf dress, only
to shimmy it off.

FOREST FOR THE TREES

Oaks are immobile
at your eye-level. Above
your head, they're frantic.

IT JUST MIGHT WORK, 3 AM

Sweet sleep of reason,
hacked woods of waking. Chances?
Vanishingly small.

OPENING SENTENCE

"Women in the dark
up the road, by the cornfield,
laughing, exclaiming."

SPRING AWAKENING DANCE RECITAL

You were Peter Pan,
while the parts of the Lost Boys
were played by Lost Girls.

SINGIN' IN THE RAIN/LES PARAPLUIES DE CHERBOURG

The heart's passe-partout,
the heart's parkour. Glorious
Technicolor tears.

Demy's umbrella
in the horizontal rain:
One teary eyelash.

NOSTALGIE

Red diaper babies!
Red-letter day at the dead
metaphor office.

KIDS' MENU

Bons mots? No, burnt toast.
Aperçus? No, apple juice.
The fingers of fish??

ASTRAY

The lines of this poem:
Strict horizontals, end stop.
Stylized subway map.

BODICE RIPPER

Curled-lip acanthus.
Crinoline adrenaline!
She slammed the book shut.

SHRED-IT

Names, reputations,
parmesan, cheddar, gruyère,
ripped tights, that red stain.

ETOBICOKE BUS BAY STRUT

Rain cannot dampen
the pigeons of Islington.
Party, platform 5!

YOU'VE CHANGED

Barefoot on the deck.
Spring starts February 1?
The confused heart blooms.

FLAWED THAW

Magnolia buds
and I snowed over: my fave
annihilation.

SONGBIRD

Robins trill outdoors.
I open our cage windows.
The house hums along.

SUNRISE WITH SEA MONSTERS

Storm-seer Turner
had himself lashed to a mast.
The Sirens stared back.

Communion

Here I am, a thinly veiled excuse,
piety prettied in a party dress,
a child bride among child brides.
Doe-eyed at the window, itself a doe's eye,
rimmed with cold grey velvet stone.
The wafer tastes like nothing I've known.
White patent shatters the robin's shell.
Spring unhatched from hurt pastel.

One more spring. Damned dried everlastings
clustered in The Storefront of Lost Things.
Windows grimly veiled with lace.
My tongue's perfect recall of your taste.
Street grit. The zippered gleam of my high-
heeled boots, the reflection in my drink-bright eyes.
Oh, the velvet rub of that ribboned frock.
A white flocked dress that strayed from the flock.

Chrysoprase

With you, the dawning awareness at dusk
of chalcedony, chrysoprase,

in the pendant your cheekbone brushed aside
as you kissed down to my left breast's swerve.

The opalescent film on the window:
adularescence by day—yearn from blue to grey.

Our anywhere room: hotel in Singapore, house in Thunder Bay,
boathouse on the moon. A taste to disambiguate,

that saltwater pearl under my tongue.
Pink and blue eyeshadow sky

led to chatoyancy by night:
the black cat's eye, blackout flashlight.

Legacy

A cracked amethyst geode glows by your bed,
miniature peak scaled for childhood dreams,
trucked over highways to rest near your head.

Not for your bedside a sterling rattle,
pink anime pony with neon hair
or microchipped gnome of grin and babble.

You'll count rough facets with a small finger,
understand purple before you say "purple,"
crawl into crystal fractures and linger.

Raw like contractions, raw like the moon.
Unashamed purple: my passion for you
and this unwieldy treasure. I'll leave too soon.

Rich

The graf kid spilled silver,
a rich surge, an ache,
when he signed his name wildstyle,
licking the bridge.
Like splotches on dropcloth
the spray fell to earth,
silver-leafing the leaves
by the silted river.

We met under the bridge.
You steepled my nipple.
Our unspoken names
swelled into each other.
The river ran silver.
My breast's arch emblazoned,
so rich. Your Midas touch
stopped my heart gold.

The Pavement

The pavement's a ladder that fell to the Earth,
A row of stale biscuits, a concrete-spread bed.
The pavement's a gingerbread door for a witch
Who wakes at your footsteps and curses your head.

The pavement's a map to the Land of Disgust.
The pavement's a noticeboard splattered with blood.
Sugared with snow crystals, peppered with tears.
A rug for a cat. A rooftop in a flood.

The pavement is well known for leading you on,
For just lying there while you do all the work.
The pavement goes right where you need it?
Oh, no. It ends in the middle. It's cracked. It's a jerk.

The pavement is how I will make my escape.
I'll run, then I'll walk, then I'll crawl, then I'll creep.
The pavement's the very first place where we kissed.
The place where your tongue, my heart took their last leap.

Fortuna

Curfew in the flowers' feverhouse:
September. The after-heat leaving the bar.

The glow that snaked around our ankles
as we passed Psychic Tyche's shuttered shop.

Praying gables of Victorian semis. Brick dust
in night air. Storefronts from Hopper.

Strings of lights tangled like sleep-tousled hair
in apartments where music throbs. Rooms not ours.

Flame-orange DETOUR. Descent to the Underworld.
Blear-eyed lights, the subway's menacing breath.

Our half-swallowed talk as we spoke to the tracks.
Dark tunnel over your left, my right.

The roar, inevitable. All I heard were your eyes.
Your hand in my hair. Derailed by your kiss.

~

We will never exit that stage-set park.
Coyote and fox, city-embedded.

I'm sunburnt by your moonlit stubble.
Boughs bent to bows. Arrows pulled from my side.

I stab my fingers into your mouth.
Artemis trains dogs on our hides.

45

Boyish, you reached up to unhook a leaf,
like a near star, to slick your torso clear.

I'll search for that perfumed ghost until dawn.
I want to burn it into my thigh.

~

Our owl-eyed driver turns his head, not his gaze.
The inverse metre of our hour counts up.

News rages on screen. Your hands cloak mine.
We must hurry our sun across the streets.

Phoebus smuggled in our day of night.
A fortune teller's orb cracked by heat.

Those Pretty Wrongs

Your open eye is an underwater sunrise.
A shower of gold bees, a pollen cloud,
that's you to me. No need to trouble
the hive mind—you'll be the first to know.

My pigeon-blood ruby, my travelling ruby,
my star-of-India found on the street.
I carry you in a fitted velvet case.
My blush betrays what I mean to tell.

The map is greedy, ink bites the page
and tears off roofs. It's a Category Four,
our fevered wish. The satellite dish
and the satellite must weep for their decay.

This theatre has 200 lolling tongues.
We perch on two. Light closes her eyes.
The dark yawns at the pregnant pause.
Then there's our story up on screen:

meet-cute, then heist, dystopia,
rom-com, subtitled documentary,
a Bollywood epic, the last Western.
Any arrows from the audience?

I have one heel spiked in the streetcar track.
Flamingoed. You lift me out of my shoe.
We are flagrant. We force a swerve.
We are the storm in the drivers' eyes.

That genie—he's not going back in the lamp.
He's unrolled the carpets, flung down the pillows,
folded his arms, and now smoke's Isadoring
to inner space. How to breathe, swallow, not choke.

We are soaking in lust, splashing in love's shallows.
I'm naked under your sweater. Books turn their backs.
I'm naked on stage under "Surprise Pink" gel.
Naked in heels here on the street corner,

all shivers when you grip my arm for attention,
then slip your mouth under my fall of hair
to whisper the last line a lick below my jaw,
all my emotions, neck and neck.

That list of beds in a history of design.
The gilded arrowhead headboard.
I had to stop reading, slam shut my eyes.
All dark scheming, my surging thoughts.

Figuring, handspan, depth and bounce.
How we would trounce those beds to disrepair.
Every way you'd pierce. Lie down with me
across the world. Pillow talk under this quiver.

When you leap from the page
or laugh through the screen
with your doubter's mouth—hey, come here!
I want to untwist it with a kiss.

That's enough of your lip.
It will never be enough.
We're a three-ring circus. We are cut ups.
My. goodness. mister. I'm in pieces.

We met where accidents start or end:
on the cold shoulder of the road.
Now I want to charm you.
I want to snake charm you.

The metal hit the bell at the top.
I said your name like an accusation,
a sweet accusation. We're live-wiring. Hot wired.
At first, we hummed. Now we hurricane.

Clearly, I like to be impossible.
I like impossibilities. I keep my eyes open.
And here's what I did
(*had to do, had to tell you*)

I curled up on one side,
held the bed's edge
and said, said your name,
hair half over my face.

Our field of honour a bed of thorns.
Scarlet letters below my footfalls.
The A my child carved into an apple.
I cannot bar you from my dreams

where it's always dawn under mulberries,
every hedgerow sings your song,
fire streaks from a rock, our skin's pearlescent.
This hallucination might be all there is.

Not California

The shadows are wrong; the leaves, starlets:
unsteady on their stems, serrated smiles.

A glimpse of water like an answer, answer, answer.
Perfume pouts. Won't leave the bed.

Noir, your eyes. Your hair, seal-sleek.
I run the rushes in my head.

Competing sweetnesses: ferns, chlorine.
That once meant war. Summer, now.

Addict of next. *Inebriate of air.*
It's morning here and last night there.

A Méliès moon. *I want I want.*
Phoebe, kick the daylights out.

The Year of La Jetée

Three fingers of moon in the glass.
Enumerate, illumine me.
We haven't hit the threshold yet.
Light shoots from the lip.

Light has every intention.
I was born in black and white.
I cradle my head to expose the film.
The year of *La jetée*.

I was born in black and white.
Your year went psychedelic.
The troubled year of the White Album,
every colour but none.

You thought those songs were full of ghosts
when you were twenty-six.
Now you must sing those ghosts to sleep.
And they've never heard of sleep.

Hey, Blackbird, I'll bring the ice
if you promise to sing until it melts.
I'm not a girl who misses much,
dressed as I am for the comeback.

What would we do without the basement and attic,
the id and superego of the house?
Tell me, assembled phantasms,
would we finally get some sleep?

In Vain

You are the ostrich plume
tickling the wind

the peacock feather
lashed to the fan

the uncarved tusk
brandished in air

the coral drops
asleep in the Aegean

the azure kingfisher
of hairpin heartstops

the frost-tipped sable
rippling over shoulders

the amber tortoiseshell
riding mirrored waves.

You are, unadorned,
rare and adored.

Well made, well wrought.
Cruelly gone.

If Wishes Were Houses

Too damn hot in the house of pillows.
The house of shame, of absent host.
The house of *Who's your daddy* and
The house of wholly ghost.

The house of cards, the house of shards,
The house of claws and teeth.
The house of walking backwards and
The house that lies beneath.

The house that never lets you.
The house of velvet gown.
The house of barely scraping by.
The house of burning down.

   I wish I'd learned the chords.
   I wish I hadn't said.
   I wish I'd never met you.
   I wish we were in bed.

Valentine's Day

Cherry-bled mittens:
two halves of a heart.

Each holds your pulse.
Hug me in stereo.

The import of the rose
to a hostile climate.

Without reservations,
tables turned.

La fée verte?
I'm seeing stardust.

The Widow's emerald?
Trouble bath.

Nipples hard, forthright.
The sucker's punch.

Feathers plucked. Freeze frame.
"Going, going, swan."

They told us: If it bleeds,
it leads. We're all hearts here.

Three

Night School

I started school at *Immaculée-Conception*, if you can believe it.
If you believe that, just step this way into my chalk drawing.

The freckles splotched on bamboo are the tears of a jilted wife?
Each day I find new beauty spots emblazoned by the sun.

He loves me not, he loves me past the melting point of steel.
Every streetlight's a fixed star, a star burnt out at dawn.

Battledore and shuttlecock, hobbyhorse and peepshow.
I was a self-righting toy until you changed the rules.

Inside the glassy-eyed greenhouse, flowers amp up the heat.
Carnation, Lily, Lily, Rose. *Jeunes filles en fleur* taunt teacher.

The view from here to the earth's core is quite spectacular!
The light will slow-dance on those leaves whatever day you've had.

Beds of roses end as bubbles in the claw-foot tub.
It only takes one burning bush to set the hills on fire.

Mary Mary, quite contrary, labour movement leader.
I'll say it: Mariolatry left gorgeous stains on glass.

Maids with centre-parted hair, knights-errant in distress.
The temple is a wreck, but just think what we learned from this.

Playmates

The ice in the field has its game face on. That wind will toy with
   your feelings.
May I recommend revenge, served chilled in silence and slow time?

The toy lies upturned in the bin, wheels stilled or legs askew.
As soon as one kid palms it, the others whine in chorus.

So it is with the redhead at the bar, the blonde on your roommate's
   bed.
I've jammed your signal with sticky fingers: remote control's over
   and out.

I thought I was writing you love poems. Turns out, I was writing
   to Mars.
"Dear distant red-faced planet! How highly ironic you are."

How artless, all that sweet talk while you twisted the pocket knife.
Meretricious. A miniature elephant carved in poachers' ivory.

As soon as a child is handed a toy, he tears off the wrapper and feasts.
But then, from the corner of the room, the empty box works its magic.

Cold and perfect, the toys in the window; the smears on the glass are
   where art lies.
When your abacus is missing a bead, you learn so much more
   about math.

What Washes Off, What Sticks

The grey-clothed day unsheathes to pink. Tickles the horizon.
Nightfall on site. I rub the jaw of the daffodil-dinosaur digger.

Light makes its last, weak argument. Excuses itself for the night.
No more hearsing and rehearsing. One false note: colony collapse.

Your lack of inflection troubles me. You must seize a ghost by the
    wrist.
Is this obsession, addiction, habit or an unscratchable itch?

We need new earth, dirt bags! They're sandbagged up at the mall.
Sweet soil arrived from the countryside. Got trashed in the parkette.

The ransom note in tenor clef of nosebleed on the pavement.
The cursive curse of a love note pissed in pale ale on the snow.

Strike the set. The dream mill's strapped to a dead-pan flatbed trailer.
The coldest day in decades and the sky is newborn blue.

You scrub at the stain while marvelling at what washes off, what
    sticks.
A missed miscarriage. The heartbeat that skipped town but never left.

Reluctant, Reluctant

If "nothing less than perfection will do," you're likely in talks with
the devil.
You could prop up that régime with one foot. The Emperor never
gets dressed.

The fortunes in these cookies are all "character is destiny."
I'm surprised to find myself still on the menu. I must be there for
a reason.

A blind owl's eyes and the planet Mercury swim into my ken:
Blue unknowable jewels. I've left your tears on the shelf by the door.

In the tale of the princess and the pea, what keeps her awake is a
pearl.
A pearl smothered in mattresses, the grit at the heart of lust.

The moon is a pearl we've lost and found and lost and found and lost.
Let me in. You know my iris. I'll match you brainwave for wave.

The page wears a sliver of gold. Sackcloth smothers the hedge in winter.
A thorn from that hedge will prick you and spit rubies in the snow.

Reluctant, Reluctant, let down your long hair! The offer has almost
expired.
So wise, the swans, doubling back their necks to sleep on their own
featherbeds.

The Coin Under the Leftmost Sliding Cup

Did you feel the Earth move? That was our Tectonic Dance Party.
The world is a crowded club with all the exits blocked.

I might sound like a goose in an opera gown, but I say again,
   I love you.
I'm tired of all this thinking at the very top of my lungs.

If only my fingers could keep up! Then the dialogue in my head
wouldn't unscroll like a '30s screwball in underwater slo-mo.

What if the truth of desire lies in Aesop upside down?
Where the fox's teeth are the Unattainable, and the grapes full of
   rationalizations…

I'm not too cool to care, though. Nature and I have a lovers' quarrel.
I adopted the strut of the peacock and the nightingale's nightgown.

After 15,000 texts, can we say we have a past?
My love for you is e-phemeral, elliptical, ekphrastic.

Love to me was cotton candy: spangle, collapse, tongue grit.
With you, it's sadness scissored out. Lights on a suspension bridge.

Sport with me. I am the coin under the leftmost sliding cup.
Right, left, double-crossing…There. Now you're in *my* pocket.

Cellphone, psalter, cigarette, gun: we like to set fire to our palms.
Rome burns as I photograph flowers or wear them as a bra.

Call it playing with fire. Call it connect-the-dots lightning.
Whenever we run down to the lake, the lake ascends sky mountain.

Streetlight's an earthbound lunatic, courting June's too-perfect
  leaves.
These gardens are a *plein-air* perfume factory, drunk on their own
  power.

The Spaceman loved the Gumball Machine (*beautiful, beautiful*).
But each time he took her by the arm, she lost another sweet eye.

It's curtains for you, day. Stars eye us from the stage.
Ars longa, vita brevis, kid. Long walk, short pier.

Makeshift Memorial

How to "pack light"? Darkness overflows from every carry-on.
While you live, you're packing heat. And then the cold sets in.

Gather ye rosebuds, rock star. Go on, sword-swallow the pretties.
Fringed skirts flash in the prison-yard lights of the used car lot.

The dog attends His Master's Voice; the cat's a turntablist.
Yes, yes, rain looks like tears. It sounds like laughter in the gutter.

My pattern of behaviour is obvious? Then solve my Rubik's mood.
Run down that clock, little mouse, and whisker '1 am.'

Toes off the sustain pedal. Bass back in the case.
We had to cut our love tour short at the wistful terminus.

We tore the gauze of the ozone, ripped the veil from the butterflies.
The screen is our eternal flame, our festive firelog channel.

The walls have ears now deafened by the soundtrack of our lives:
The adenoidal buzz of the common house fly and the faltering
    storefront sign.

I'm speaking from dead centre of a southbound arctic air mass.
Warm, warmer…Bye, ice floes…They left on a jet plane.

When you left, I took my temperature to peace talks in Geneva.
Oh, to be your split second! Not your makeshift memorial.

The Headless Long-Stemmed Rose on a
Staircase in the Subway

The Master of the Large Foreheads is restless at the Frick.
In my beautiful lapis blue gown, I hailed a silkworm south on Fifth.

Orpheus, mute, on a gilt salt cellar. That's his lot in life.
Each afternoon, from the subway singer: "Another day in hell…"

Not every sidewalk musician's an undiscovered Joshua Bell.
But each one plays your heartstrings with a quaver of regret.

You did yourself a party favour and unzipped my dress.
A lab-made opal ring pulled the film over my eyes.

I intend to pit general knowledge against specific gravity.
Nature struggles to learn from itself. Meanwhile, we're gunning it.

Peach-ache of ripeness: a beard in the throat. Pewter ware is "sadware."
All I am is a pewter plate melted down for musket balls.

Planters crammed with chrysanthemums are the burial mounds of
    summer.
Even after death, cut sunflowers send up signal flares.

Nothing like the sound of your plane leaving and leaving and leaving.
Whenever I wish you *Good Morning*, it's the living end of *Good Night*.

To Kateri Tekakwitha of the Kanien'kehá:ka

(from a settler poet baptized with her name)

"Lily of the Mohawks." A bed of thorns for Kateri.
Otsi'tsa—flower; otsi'tsa'shon:'a—flowers. Small-pox survivor, Kateri.

Cohen's *Beautiful Losers*, mass cards, prayer cards, medallions,
wax effigies, stone statues claimed your image, Kateri.

The "Highway of Tears" is a continent-wide slash.
The missing women, never found…Where to leave flowers, Kateri?

The thistle, shamrock, rose, the dagger-petalled fleur-de-lis.
"To plant lilies on the graves of the Iroquois." The governor's wish, Kateri.

My mother's covenant: "If my sister lives, I'll name a daughter 'Kateri.'"
I've seen your tomb, a block of snow, a press of lilies, Kateri.

Is this ghazal a rosary, a siren's wail, a karen:in?
We left the church, my parents and I—I grieve its harm, Saint Kateri.

Kateri Tekakwitha, I spell your name into the world
with awkward love. My years'-long wish: To hear your story, Kateri.

Only Rain

I

I'll be rushing, the way I do. Before the door slams. Half in love
    with vertigo.
You were the unforeseen, uninvited, un-be-lieve-able and now
    undoable.

On a parchment fragment, the corner torn, you've tied my hair in
    Celtic knots.
Time sinks, synchs and then you're down to edges of light around
    the door.

Light from the southwest strikes between the eyes. Magic hour mocks,
    clicks the link.
You're a jagged halo just getting through. Cabinet of curiosities left
    unlocked.

In the experiment, we are immersed in water. Left on twin hilltops.
    Denied electricity.
How many seasons must I wait? This snow tests positive for
    crystallized tears.

II

I lie along the lakeshore, breasts to the embankment. Longing as
    long as the clanging harbour.
Pressed against the wharfs, I curl my legs. I was a dancing girl.
    How did I dream here?

With a rake of light along my curves, I've become the industrial
    shoreline.
Water sluices my iron and concrete. What are we to do? *My dame
has lost her shoe.*

Over my shoulder's a view of lake haze, dance halls of the '20s,
    yachts in hauteur.
Long-haired willows weep for the mainland. Platinum waves loll
    on the beach.

The islands—I could swim there in three strokes! Wind in the
    leaves, that rainless rain sound.
In the tunnel, stare-lights of cars. The expressway's roar of
    disapproval.

Condo sites shed great glass tears, bids for attention fallen flat.
The arrowhead shards land near my eyes. Their leaves of glass my
    blades in sand.

Every word of ours is freighted. Let's row our archaisms to sea.
Here's our sieve and our crockery jar. I'm the figurehead fallen
    from your tall ship.

Mixed messages, font corrupted at birth. The bare and throbbing
    fontanel.
I'm a mother with a riven heart. Molten, hollowed out, riveted.

You lift the hair at my nape. *We know too well.* Pleasure longs to
    drown, blacks out.
But I am floating past your reach. Little boats pull me through
rough
    waves.

I'm a swan on the bank, dropping red petals. After you left I took
    the hurricane inside.
When I spit it out, it's only rain. *For still temptation follows where
    thou art.*

III

Stripped tree the marker. I'll turn and find you. At once:
everything we meant to say.
Hourglass hills, wine glass on its side. Inward-flaming rose, this
garden enclosed.

Wetter than tears the slip of your tongue. Wet earth the base note,
the bass line.
The sever now sutured, the fountain sealed. We shiver into one
another.

Your driving kiss. *We meant to say.* In the sudden dark, I can
barely see the road.
But I accelerate. And only for you would I dissolve. Would I
drink the pearl and find it sweet.

NOTES

"Merrily, Merrily, Merrily, Merrily" quotes a song from Shakespeare's *As You Like It*.

"There Was Something In My Dream About a Cat" takes, as its title, a line from John Berryman's Dream Song 25. The poem also quotes a song from Shakespeare's *The Tempest*.

"Uncontrolled Burn" rings a change on Philip Larkin's line: "What will survive of us is love" in "An Arundel Tomb."

"Easy Street" quotes the General Prologue to The Canterbury Tales by Geoffrey Chaucer.

"Florillegal" quotes the Wikipedia entry on forget-me-nots from fall 2013.

"Heart Monitor" is haunted by Whitman, Browning, Blake, Dickinson, Munch and Vermeer. I owe a debt of gratitude to them for their words and paintings and to the doctors at Sunnybrook Health Sciences Centre in Toronto.

"A Colder Spring" quotes Hamlet's soliloquy in Act 1, Scene 2.

"Emerald Table" has, as an epigraph, the first line of the ancient text known as the Emerald Tablet or Table (regarded as the primary text in alchemy and Hermetics). Sir Isaac Newton's translation of the Latin reads: Tis true without lying, certain & most true. Newton's translation of line 7 of the text forms lines 13-14 of the poem. Lines 8-9 of the poem are from the Paolo and Francesca passage in Dante's *Inferno* (Canto V, lines 121-123).

"Those Pretty Wrongs" takes, as its title, part of a line from Shakespeare's Sonnet 41. Another line from Sonnet 41 is quoted in the poem "Only Rain."

"Not California" quotes #214 by Emily Dickinson ("I taste a liquor never brewed"). It also makes a reference to early French filmmaker Georges Méliès, whose most famous film is "A Trip to the Moon" ("Le Voyage dans la Lune").

"In Vain" quotes John Skelton's "To Mistress Margaret Hussey."

"Night School" mentions "Carnation, Lily, Lily, Rose," which is the title of a painting by John Singer Sargent. The title of that painting came from a line in a popular song, "Ye Shepherds Tell Me," by the British composer Joseph Mezzinghi.

"To Kateri Tekakwitha of the Kanien'kehá:ka" draws on a speech by Darren Bonaparte, "A Lily Among Thorns: The Mohawk Repatriation of Káteri Tekahkwí:tha," presented at the 30th Conference on New York State History, JUNE 5, 2009 in Plattsburgh, N.Y. Please see wampumchronicles.com for more details and for information on Darren Bonaparte's book by the same title.

ACKNOWLEDGEMENTS

Many of the poems, some in slightly different versions, first appeared in the following print or online journals and anthologies. My thanks to the editors.

Moss Trill, Great Lakes Review, Green Mountains Review, Hazlitt, EVENT, Canadian Gingers (ed. Kim Clark and Dawn Kresan, Oolichan, 2017), *The Hood* (www.lynncrosbie.com), *Canadian Poetries, PoetrySky, Drifting Down the Lane* (ed. Agnes Marton and Harriet Lawlor, Moon and Mountain, 2013), *LyreLyre, The Literary Review of Canada, Leveler, Truck, The Fiddlehead, Arc, The Walrus, The Best of* Walrus *Poetry, Best Canadian Poetry 2014* (ed. Sonnet L'Abbé, Molly Peacock and Anita Lahey, Tightrope Books).

"The Coin Under the Leftmost Sliding Cup" won the 2013 Walrus Poetry Prize.

"To the Headless Long-stemmed Rose on a Staircase in the Subway" won third prize in the 2016 Troubadour International Poetry contest.

"Reluctant, Reluctant" was shortlisted for Arc's Poem of the Year 2016 and was an Editor's Choice in that contest.

I am grateful to the Canada Council for the Arts for a travel grant that enabled me to attend the Troubadour prize evening in London, England, October 31, 2016.

Love and thanks to Gregory, Nicholas, Julia and William Sinclair.

My thanks, for their comments on drafts of the poems, to Robert Pinsky, Richard Greene, Tanis MacDonald and the Garretians, Dan Chelotti, Kateri Akiwenzie-Damm, Mike Blouin, and James Arthur.

My thanks, for their literary and moral support, to Eduardo C. Corral, Kitty McKay Lewis, Alexander Cigale, Micheline Maylor, Alex Nagel,

Souvankham Thammavongsa, Michael Prior, Phoebe Wang, Andrew Brooks, Megan Williams, Barbara Garrick, Ariel Gordon, Gary Barwin, Virginia Konchan, David Case, Anne-Marie Fyfe, and Bruce Meyer. Thanks to Anna Yin for her translation of "Guanyin Lamp" into Chinese for the journal *PoetrySky*.

Many thanks to Glyn Maxwell and Jane Yeh for kind words and drinks in London.

My deepest thanks to everyone at Véhicule Press, to David Drummond for his stunning cover and to my superb editor, Carmine Starnino.

Signal
EDITIONS

Carmine Starnino, Editor
Michael Harris, Founding Editor

ARABY Eric Ormsby
WORDS THAT WALK IN THE NIGHT Pierre Morency
    (Translated by Lissa Cowan and René Brisebois)
A PICNIC ON ICE: SELECTED POEMS Matthew Sweeney
HELIX: NEW AND SELECTED POEMS John Steffler
HERESIES: THE COMPLETE POEMS OF ANNE WILKINSON, 1924-1961
    Edited by Dean Irvine
CALLING HOME Richard Sanger
FIELDER'S CHOICE Elise Partridge
MERRYBEGOT Mary Dalton
MOUNTAIN TEA Peter Van Toorn
AN ABC OF BELLY WORK Peter Richardson
RUNNING IN PROSPECT CEMETERY Susan Glickman
MIRABEL Pierre Nepveu (Translated by Judith Cowan)
POSTSCRIPT Geoffrey Cook
STANDING WAVE Robert Allen
THERE, THERE Patrick Warner
HOW WE ALL SWIFTLY: THE FIRST SIX BOOKS Don Coles
THE NEW CANON: AN ANTHOLOGY OF CANADIAN POETRY
    Edited by Carmine Starnino
OUT TO DRY IN CAPE BRETON Anita Lahey
RED LEDGER Mary Dalton
REACHING FOR CLEAR David Solway
OX Christopher Patton
THE MECHANICAL BIRD Asa Boxer
SYMPATHY FOR THE COURIERS Peter Richardson
MORNING GOTHIC: NEW AND SELECTED POEMS George Ellenbogen
36 CORNELIAN AVENUE Christopher Wiseman
THE EMPIRE'S MISSING LINKS Walid Bitar
PENNY DREADFUL Shannon Stewart
THE STREAM EXPOSED WITH ALL ITS STONES D.G. Jones
PURE PRODUCT Jason Guriel
ANIMALS OF MY OWN KIND Harry Thurston
BOXING THE COMPASS Richard Greene
CIRCUS Michael Harris
THE CROW'S VOW Susan Briscoe
WHERE WE MIGHT HAVE BEEN Don Coles
MERIDIAN LINE Paul Bélanger (Translated by Judith Cowan)
SKULLDUGGERY Asa Boxer
SPINNING SIDE KICK Anita Lahey
THE ID KID Linda Besner
GIFT HORSE Mark Callanan
SUMPTUARY LAWS Nyla Matuk
THE GOLDEN BOOK OF BOVINITIES Robert Moore
MAJOR VERBS Pierre Nepveu (Translated by Donald Winkler)
ALL SOULS' Rhea Tregebov
THE SMOOTH YARROW Susan Glickman
THE GREY TOTE Deena Kara Shaffer
HOOKING Mary Dalton
DANTE'S HOUSE Richard Greene
BIRDS FLOCK FISH SCHOOL Edward Carson
THE SCARBOROUGH Michael Lista
RADIO WEATHER Shoshanna Wingate
LAWS & LOCKS Chad Campbell
LEAVING THE ISLAND Talya Rubin
INSTALLATIONS David Solway
MOCKINGBIRD Derek Webster
LATE VICTORIANS Vincent Colistro
MODEL DISCIPLE Michael Prior
BASED ON ACTUAL EVENTS Robert Moore
STRANGER Nyla Matuk
SIREN Kateri Lanthier
TABLE MANNERS Catriona Wright